50 THINGS TO KNOW ABOUT BIRDS IN INDIANA

Birds in
the Crossroads
of America

Rachel Horon

Cover designed by: Ivana Stamenkovic
Cover Image: pixabay

CZYK Publishing Since 2011.
CZYKPublishing.com
50 Things to Know

Lock Haven, PA
All rights reserved.
ISBN: 9798495239173

50 THINGS TO KNOW
ABOUT BIRDS IN THE USA

If you know someone who loves birds, I cannot imagine them not learning or enjoying this book.

This book is perfect for both experienced birders and beginners alike. It is written in readable prose and studded with personal stories from the author's many years of observing birds.

50 Things to Know About Birds in Pennsylvania: Birding in the Keystone State
Author Darryl & Jackie Speicher

I really enjoyed this book. I live in the Badger state and I learned a lot of things I didn't know before. The author got me excited about taking up bird watching. Definitely going to plan a day trip to Horicon Marsh.

50 Things to Know About Birds in Wisconsin : Birding in the Badger State
Author Carly Lincoln

50 THINGS TO KNOW ABOUT BIRDS IN INDIANA

BOOK DESCRIPTION

Do you want to know about the amazing birds found in Indiana? Do you want to know where to find them and be able to identify them? If you answered yes to any of these questions then this book is for you...

50 Things to Know About Birds in Indiana by author Rachel Horon offers an approach to bird watching specifically in Indiana. Most books on birds tell you scientific details about different species. Although there's nothing wrong with that, this book is one that will interest all levels of bird watchers and enthusiasts. Based on knowledge from the world's leading experts and local insiders, you will discover interesting facts and stories about Indiana birds.

In these pages you'll discover new places to visit and the common and unique birds that call Indiana home, even if temporarily. This book will help you discover your own places to find migrant and backyard species in the state.

By the time you finish this book, you will know more about the most common backyard bird as well as the fierce birds of prey. So grab YOUR copy today. You'll be glad you did.

TABLE OF CONTENTS

DEDICATION

"No bird soars too high if he soars with his own wings."

\- William Blake

I could not have accomplished my dreams of becoming a writer without the support and motivation of many people. However, my first dedication is promised to Conrad Noll, IV. It has been over 4 years since you encouraged me to write my books and get them published. Thank you for believing in me.

I also want to acknowledge my best friend Jen Deimel. Just like when we proofread the other person's history papers in college, I am glad that she could help me out again with this project.

ABOUT THE AUTHOR

Rachel Horon is an author for the young and the young at heart. Originally from Illinois, she became a Hoosier through marriage. Twenty years and two teenagers later, Rachel and her family live on their wooded property surrounded by backyard wildlife.

She has worn many hats in her career starting as her childhood dream to be a teacher. Her love for reading took her out of the classroom and into her own published works. Rachel has published a series of digital books for Smart Kidz Club, an app that connects children to a digital library for early and elementary readers. She also collaborated with Jamie Stonebridge in a collection of senior fiction on Amazon.

Find her on social media at:

Facebook: https://www.facebook.com/rachelhoronauthor

Instagram: @rhoron https://insights.bookbub.com/great-author-bio-examples

INTRODUCTION

"A bird does not sing because it has an answer,
it sings because it has a song."

-Maya Angelou

Why do people watch birds? We are mesmerized by their ease in flight, their power in the hunt, and their beauty enrobed in feathers. Our eyes are drawn to the majestic eagle and the curious seagull, but also the common birds that are found in many backyards.

At the same time, we are drawn by their songs. They call us to their perch, alert us to activity in the grass, or just sing their song. Bird watchers never look for answers when they come across a feathered creature, but they find so much more.

Indiana has its fair share of aviary wonders. While many are right in a Hoosier's backyard, anyone who visits the Crossroads of America can join in with local experts or follow a song on their own. From Lake Michigan to the Ohio River, this book will give you 50 things you should know about the birds of Indiana.

MOST COMMON BACKYARD BIRDS

https://pixabay.com/photos/bird-redbird-cardinal-songbird-5357194/

1. NORTHERN CARDINAL

In 1933, the cardinal was designated Indiana's state bird. This non-migratory bird with its distinctive crest and red feathers can be seen all over the state, particularly in the central region. The female has the same crest but brown feathers. The male and female cardinal mate for life and are a symbol of love and hope.

Street names, businesses, and sports mascots are just a few entities that use the name and image of this bird. Charlie Cardinal is the mascot for Ball State University in Muncie, Indiana. A cardinal

Did You Know?

The cardinal gets its bright red feathers from the foods they eat. The pigments from the grapes and dogwood berries that they find to eat go through their bloodstream to their feather follicles.

https://pixabay.com/photos/robin-american-robin-redbreast-bird-3159166/

2. AMERICAN ROBIN

"Today is the day when bold kites fly,

When cumulus clouds roar across the sky.

When robins return, when children cheer,

When light rain beckons spring to appear."

- Robert McCracken

The robin is a sign of spring, but they are actually found in Indiana year-round. This ground forager is the early bird pecking at insects and worms in the soil. At the same time, you can spy them in the trees when you look for their orange breast.

They will enjoy some of the offerings in backyard bird feeders, especially when they make their presence known at the beginning of spring. Sweet treats like fruits or berries are also on their menu, but fermented berries can make them appear to be intoxicated.

https://pixabay.com/photos/dove-bird-animal-perched-6168339/

3. MOURNING DOVE

The mourning dove is also a ground forager, but is more interested in seeds than in insects. They can store their seed finds in their crop, an enlarged part of their esophagus. That gives them the option to enjoy their food at a later time. When they are holding on to those seeds, their breasts will get more round as they expand.

There is an abundance of mourning doves in backyards and the forests, but they tend to enjoy perching on telephone wires in neighborhoods. The eyes on their small head keeps an eye out for their next meal.

Did You Know?

The mourning dove gets its name from the lamentful sound of its coos and calls.

https://pixabay.com/photos/bird-bluejay-wildlife-nature-jay-4854855/

4. BLUE JAY

"The bluebird carries the sky on his back."

- Henry David Thoreau.

Where there are acorns, there are blue jays. In fact, they are credited for the abundance of oak trees. Just like squirrels, the blue jay hides acorns for the winter. These birds are smart like their crow cousins and will remember many of their hiding places. However, they will miss a few and the result is oak saplings come spring.

While their bird calls are noisy to some, their screeches, similar to a hawk's, may alert other birds to predators in the area.

Blue jays are known for their striking feather colors and black bridle across their face and nape. This may help birds recognize each other in their tight family groups. However, their feathers are not blue. Their wings have pockets of air and keratin. When the sun shines on their feathers, all of the colors of the wavelength are absorbed except for blue. That is reflected in what is called light scattering.

https://pixabay.com/photos/bird-american-goldfinch-beak-5607116/

5. AMERICAN GOLDFINCH

A flash of gold in the air may be an American goldfinch. In spring, the males have the brightest plumage but the females and goldfinches in the other seasons are just as easy to see. Their conical bills are used for gleaning seeds and other small bits of food from leaves and the ground. You may see them flipping fallen leaves in search of morsels. However, milkweed thistle is one of their favorite plants for nest building and as a food source.

A flock of goldfinches are called a charm. These birds are very social and will flock together as soon as breeding is through for the season. Breeding occurs later in the season, as in they do not start breeding until late June.

Did You Know?

An American goldfinch pair makes almost identical calls.

https://pixabay.com/photos/downy-woodpecker-woodpecker-bird-6342485/

6. DOWNY WOODPECKER

There are six species of woodpeckers that live in Indiana year round. The smallest of the birds is the downy woodpecker. They do not grow to be more than 7 inches in length, almost the same size as the chickadees and nuthatches that they feed with. One reason that they may stay close to other flocks is for protection from predators.

The black-and-white woodpecker with tiny red tufts on their crown uses their size to their advantage in other ways. Compared to their larger cousins, the downy woodpecker can feed from weeds such as goldenrod. Insects and their larvae can be abundant for them. They also enjoy suet feeders in backyards.

Did You Know?

When it comes to hammering on a tree, woodpeckers have special feathers around their nostrils to keep them from breathing in wood chips.

https://pixabay.com/photos/woodpecker-red-bellied-woodpecker-5429886/

7. RED-BELLIED WOODPECKER

Another common Indiana woodpecker is the red-bellied woodpecker. The stripe pattern on their wings and back along with the bright red cap on their heads helps bird watchers identify them.

They feast on insects as well as nuts and seeds. One way that these woodpeckers attract mates is by making loud noises not including their bird calls. Males have been known to tap metal gutters and aluminum roofs to get the attention of females.

Woodpeckers benefit trees by eating the insects and pests that can damage trees. Their strong beaks can drill into the trunk, but their brains are protected by the bones that actually absorb the shocks and vibrations. Their long sticky tongue, almost 2 inches in length past the end of the beak, helps protect their brain as well as reaches deep into bark nooks and crannies.

Did You Know?

The cartoon character Woody Woodpecker was inspired by an annoying yet persistent woodpecker. Even though Woody has a red cap like a red-bellied woodpecker, it may have been an acorn woodpecker.

https://pixabay.com/photos/tufted-titmouse-bird-wood-snow-5845780/

8. TUFTED TITMOUSE

This bird has a similar silhouette compared to the cardinal, but this frequent visitor to backyard feeders has a bushy crest with a pointy tuft pointing back. Their black beak and gray feathers are a few of their stand-out features for such a small bird up to six inches long.

The tufted titmouse is part of the chickadee family and is considered non-migratory. They may still travel around their region, but they are more likely to build nests in tree cavities or nest boxes.

Since they cannot dig out their own nests in trees, they stake their claim in natural holes or dead wood cavities. Predators include snakes, raccoons, skunks and opossums, but the tufted titmouse can become aggressive during breeding season and mob against predators. Sometimes those predator's fur will become a part of their nests.

Did You Know?

The tufted titmouse got its name from the Old English words that means small bird.

https://pixabay.com/photos/white-breasted-nuthatch-bird-perched-6647446/

9.   WHITE-BREASTED NUTHATCH

The nuthatch got its name from its process for eating nuts. It sticks nuts or seeds into the tree bark, then hits it hard and frequently with its beak in order to get the meat out of it. The white-breasted nuthatch is also black and gray.

The white-breasted nuthatch uses a lot of defensive methods to survive. For example, the male does most of the foraging while the female watches his back. This pair is monogamous and will stay close together throughout the year. They also use large flocks of other backyard birds to show strength in numbers and resourcefulness for watching for predators. Since they are non-migratory, they will remain in their territory, preferably near deciduous trees.

Did You Know?

The white-breasted nuthatch has a hallux, or one big toe that is backwards, which helps the nuthatch hold on to the bark while it faces headfirst down the tree to look for bugs in the bark.

https://pixabay.com/photos/american-crow-crow-bird-wildlife-4249245/

10. AMERICAN CROW

The American crow has a presence almost all over the country including Indiana. These omnivores can find food anywhere from bird feeders to roadsides. Their black feathers have a reflective sheen that makes them even more noticeable in the sunlight. Their large groups, referred to as "murders", flock around food sources or offer protection from potential threats.

The crow is associated with trickery and death, but also great intelligence. In Aesop's fable "The Crow and the Pitcher", the thirsty crow figured out that adding pebbles to a pitcher with just a little bit of water made the water level rise close to his beak. They have also learned how to adapt in more locations, even urban developments.

NOTABLE BIRDS

https://pixabay.com/photos/heron-great-blue-heron-5337163/

11. GREAT BLUE HERON

The Great Blue Heron is the largest heron. The bird stands tall with its long legs and s-shaped neck in blue-gray shades. This large wading bird lives in marshes where their fish is plentiful. While bird watchers may enjoy watching them during daylight hours, the Great Blue also has excellent night vision for hunting.

The Great Blue Heron built nests near Lake Michigan for over 60 years. Their rookery, or colony of nests, would be high in the trees away from ground predators such as raccoons. At the same time, their numbers would protect these nests from airborne predators like eagles and owls. Today more herons are found living in east central Indiana with over 500 nests in their colonies.

Did You Know?

The adult Great Blue Heron will stand at 4 feet tall, but only weigh about 6 pounds at the most.

https://pixabay.com/photos/sandhill-crane-mating-dance-4830984/

12. SANDHILL CRANE

Cranes are similar to the heron in their body shape and habitat, but the crane has a straight neck and shorter beaks. The sandhill crane has a 7-foot wingspan while the Great Blue Heron is as big as 6 feet. When it comes to other features, the sandhill crane has a gray body and crimson-red caps.

Sandhill cranes can travel 200 miles or more during migration, and Indiana is along the sandhill crane's migratory path. After breeding in the northern region of the continent, roughly 15,000 cranes take refuge in the prairie and marshlands of some of the state's fish and wildlife areas. Sandhill cranes mate for life.

Did You Know?

A sandhill crane fossil found in Florida is dated as about 2.5 million years old.

https://pixabay.com/photos/vulture-bird-grass-resting-708783/

13. VULTURES

There are two types of vultures in Indiana: the turkey vulture and the black vulture. They are important to the ecosystem as they clean up the environment and dispose of animal carcasses that can spread diseases.

The turkey vulture looks like its namesake with its red, bald head and black body. Since they are common in Indiana, these vultures may be easy to spot along roadsides or open fields. Other times they may be circling an area from above as they are searching for their next meal. Northern Indiana sees turkey vultures more in the summer as they will migrate south for the winter.

Both the turkey vulture and black vulture are scavengers with a taste for carrion, however the black vulture can and will hunt and kill their own fresh meat. Black vultures mate for life and have been seen year-round in southern Indiana close to the Ohio River.

Did You Know?

Black vultures can harm livestock but cannot not be harmed as they are protected according to the Migratory Bird Treaty Act.

By Mdf - Own work, CC BY-SA 3.0,
https://commons.wikimedia.org/w/index.php?curid=2091787

14. CERULEAN WARBLER

Out of the 18 species of warblers found in Indiana, one that excites bird watchers is the Cerulean warbler. The male resembles its name compared to the female whose plumage is more blue-green. These birds forage for insects often in the top canopies of forests which challenges observers even more. Binoculars make it easier to see warblers in the wild. The Cerulean warbler breeds in most of Indiana and will migrate south for winter.

The Cerulean warbler is another bird that is under protection as habitat loss is a huge concern to their population. Breeding grounds are being taken over by urban development and forest management practices are thinning out the mature canopies that make up their desired habitats. With their population decreasing and their status vulnerable, this makes their sightings in Indiana's deciduous forests even more special.

Did You Know?

Another preferred wintering location for Cerulean warblers is a coffee plantation.

By Dominic Sherony - Henslow's Sparrow (Ammodramus henslowii)Uploaded by Magnus Manske, CC BY-SA 2.0, https://commons.wikimedia.org/w/index.php?curid=21239890

15. HENSLOW'S SPARROW

Henslow's Sparrow is named after a friend of John James Audubon. John Stevens Henslow was a botanist as well as a teacher of Charles Darwin. In fact, he mentored Darwin and recommended him for the expedition to the Galapagos Islands.

Henslow's Sparrow blends in with the grassland environment they prefer. Their plumage colors of tan like the dry grass and streaks of black are great camouflage. One of the largest populations of Henslow's Sparrow comes to southeastern Indiana during spring migration. The problem is that habitat destruction is threatening their breeding grounds. The U.S. Fish and Wildlife Service has determined not to put the Henslow's sparrow on the endangered species list, but keep them as a "species of concern" as they can still benefit from concentrated conservation actions in the state.

Did You Know?

Despite their wings, they prefer to move on foot rather than fly. Their nests are also on the ground so bird watchers should look down when seeking this species.

https://pixabay.com/photos/black-neck-stilt-stilt-wader-4401356/

16. BLACK-NECKED STILT

The black-necked stilt is a bird commonly found on the western
half of the United States, particularly along California's coastline
and various wetlands. They thrive on insects and larvae found in and
around the water. Along with their distinctive black neck and white
breast, their long, thin legs are a distinctive trait. Its leg-to-body
proportion is similar to that of the flamingo.

So what does this California bird have to do with Indiana? The
black-necked stilt is considered one of the rarest birds in Indiana.
They have been observed more inland, not by Lake Michigan. Bird

watchers have reported seeing them in the wetlands areas in the southwest portion of the state. Also, they are not considered endangered. Their numbers have been on the rise.

Did You Know?

The black-necked stilt will soak its belly feathers in water on hot days to cool off. The absorbed water is carried to the nest to cool down the eggs and chicks as well.

https://pixabay.com/photos/pileated-woodpecker-woodpecker-bird-6610630/

17. PILEATED WOODPECKER

The largest woodpecker in Indiana is the pileated woodpecker. At over 19 inches long, it is easy to spot with its size and a bright red crest on its head. It prefers to live in cavities in trees and logs, especially ones that they have constructed in their unique rectangular holes. Woodpeckers help protect the forest from invasive insects and create shelters for a number of birds.

Bird watchers can look high and low, often following the woodpecker by its loud hammering sounds. Backyard watchers may find woodpeckers like the pileated woodpecker at suet feeders.

Did You Know?

The bill of the pileated woodpecker is as big as its head.

https://pixabay.com/photos/bird-s-eye-view-eagle-bird-glove-768193/

18. BALD EAGLE

"You cannot fly like an eagle with the wings of a wren."

- William Henry Hudson

The bald eagle was once on the endangered species list. However, through conservation efforts across the country and banning the pesticide DDT, they are no longer threatened as of 2007. Their protection does not just stop there. The Bald and Golden Eagle

Protection Act protects the birds, feathers, eggs, and nests as well. This means that there are more opportunities to see them in the wild, including Indiana.

Today there are numerous locations where people can observe the bald eagles at a safe distance. This includes watching the eagles soar, hunt for birds in the sky, or land in its treetop nests. Eagles prefer to be near water for access to fish. With their population still rising, it is possible to see multiple eagles at a wildlife refuge.

By Mdf - Own work, CC BY-SA 3.0,
https://commons.wikimedia.org/w/index.php?curid=2050840

19. CASPIAN TERN

There are plenty of gulls near Lake Michigan, but there are also other birds that look similar. The Caspian tern stands out from the gulls with its long body and large head with the black cap. These migratory birds pass through each season looking for rest and fish.

Many of the birds are generalized as gulls, but that is likely because of the birds' common features as they flock together. The Caspian tern looks different in flight with its angular wings and sharp-pointed tails. Terns are not quite the scavengers that gulls are, but they are both important to the food web in the lake ecosystem.

Did You Know?

The Caspian tern is the largest of the terns.

https://pixabay.com/photos/great-egret-flight-ardea-alba-wader-599205/

20. GREAT EGRET

The great egret is a large bird similar to the Great Blue heron and sandhill crane. With snow white feathers, long neck, and long, dark legs, the egret stands out on its own. These birds were threatened at one point with a demand for their feathers in ladies' fashion.

Through protection of their habitats and with the Migratory Bird Treaty Act, their rookeries are protected and their numbers are on the rise. Their nesting grounds can be found in parts of Northwest Indiana as well as near the Ohio River to the south.

Did You Know?

The egret is the symbol of the National Audubon Society, the bird organization established to protect birds like the great egret.

https://pixabay.com/photos/peregrine-falcon-falcon-3023839/

21. PEREGRINE FALCON

When it comes to powerful flight and fast dives, the peregrine falcon is a fine example of these traits. As they fly for travel, their speed ranges from 25-34 mph. In pursuit of prey, their flight can reach 69 mph. It is their dive, however, that is most impressive at 200 mph. From their aerial perch to the ground, their skill is impressive in the bird world.

Sightings of the peregrine falcon in Indiana are rare, but not impossible. After the species was endangered from DDT poisoning, they regained in numbers and have adapted to urban life or wetland living. These birds of prey will perch high on either skyscrapers or coastal cliffs. Migrant birds may be found in designated wildlife areas, but some falcons may be found nesting in Indianapolis, Fort Wayne, or Gary.

Did You Know?

With a diving speed of 200 mph, they are the fastest animal on the planet as well as the fastest bird.

https://pixabay.com/photos/birds-blackbirds-bobolink-nature-744778/

22. BOBOLINK

As a member of the blackbird family, the bobolink stands out from the others. The female has buff and brown feathers and a buff head, but the male stands out for mating. They have a black body and underside but their back is white. It is as if they are wearing a tuxedo to a date but put it on backwards.

Bobolinks are more common in the northern part of Indiana where the grasslands provide food like seeds and nesting grounds in the grass. However, early hay-cutting threatens their nests before they migrate south for the winter.

Did You Know?

The bobolink has one of the longest migrations in the bird world. One round-trip migration can take 12,500 miles to complete.

By Dick Daniels (http://carolinabirds.org/) - Own work, CC BY-SA 3.0, https://commons.wikimedia.org/w/index.php?curid=11117475

23. LEAST TERN

The Least Tern is the smallest of the terns. Many are found on the Atlantic coastline, but there is a population of "interior" Least Terns that live and nest near the waterways in Indiana. These inland terns were listed as endangered in 1985, but were recently removed from the Endangered Species List in 2021.

These small birds are also very protective of their territory. Watchers can distinguish them by their black and white feather patterns on their heads, but must give them plenty of distance. They are nicknamed "strikers" because they will dive to grab fish or ward off intruders to their nesting grounds. Beaches may be roped off to protect nesting colonies or protect beachgoers from hostile attacks.

Did You Know?

Least tern gets its name for being the smallest of terns. This bird should not be confused with the little tern that is found in Europe, Asia, Africa, and Australia.

https://pixabay.com/photos/malaysian-piping-plover-small-4633714/

24. PIPING PLOVER

The piping plover is a master of camouflage in the sandy habitat near Lake Michigan and the other Great Lakes. Watchers may find it challenging to find them in plain sight when their feather colors and patterns blend in so well. They are small but have a black collar and short orange bill.

These endangered birds are dealing with habitat loss, so the U.S. Fish and Wildlife Service has a critical habitat designated for them at the Indiana Dunes State Park and National Lakeshore.If spotted, they need plenty of distance. In that same area, another plover, the black-bellied plover, might be seen during migration periods.

Did You Know?

If you see a piping plover shaking one food above the wet sand, they are actually attempting to attract food from the ground. The technique called "foot trembling" is one method of foraging.

https://pixabay.com/photos/rufa-canutus-calidris-sand-red-386873/

25. RUFA RED KNOT

The Red Knot is another species living near Lake Michigan shorelines that is threatened. This member of the sandpiper family feeds on aquatic invertebrates such as horseshoe crabs or clams. They are capable of searching muddy waters for food by using the sensory organs on their bill tops.

Some distinguishing features of the red knot includes an orangy breast and face along with the tan and brown feathers on the back. Their beaks are long and rounded at the tip, ideal for shoreline fishing. They can be found as far north as the Arctic, so the best time to see a red knot is during the fall and spring migration.

Did You Know?

The rufa red knot is another long-distance migrating bird. From the High Arctic to the southern portion of South America, they are in for a one-way trip flying over 9,500 miles.

WHERE TO FIND BIRDS IN INDIANA

26. BACKYARDS

Birds are attracted to a variety of features in Indiana habitats, but it is possible to make your own backyard more inviting. Bird feeders and bird baths are two common backyard decor features that can bring more birds into view. The 10 most common backyard birds enjoy seeds and suet just as hummingbirds will seek out their specialized feeders.

Bird nesting boxes are another easy fixture in your backyard. From traditional birdhouses to boxes with cameras, bird watchers and photographers can see more of these birds. This is also to the advantage of the birds as homes for nests or shelter are in shorter supply as their habitats are dwindling.

In the summer of 2021, there was a concern about bird feeders and bird baths in Indiana. Songbirds were falling ill or dying from a mysterious illness. A bird feeder moratorium was in place until the Department of Natural Resources could identify or decrease the number of bird illnesses. At the time of publication, bird feeders are allowed to be filled again with encouragement to clean them once a week with a 10% bleach solution. The cause of illness is still unknown.

27. INDIANA DUNES NATIONAL PARK

The Indiana Dunes shoreline spans more than fifteen miles of beach and over 15,000 acres of different habitats. Wildlife is just one of the features of this national park as there are beaches, wetlands, forests, prairie, and access to the Little Calumet River. More than 350 species are found at Indiana Dunes as year-round residents or migrants passing through.

Indiana Dunes offers a variety of activities for all levels of bird watchers. Guided and self-guided bird tours are available year round. Numerous trails can take visitors to different environments in order to view different types of birds. One of their biggest organized events is the Birding Festival that takes place for one weekend in May.

The Great Blue Heron once called the Indiana Dunes Lakeshore home for over 60 years. Their rookery was accessible on the Heron Rookery Trail. While the blue heron no longer builds nests at this particular park, the trail has become home to other nesting birds such as kingfishers and warblers.

For a look at the birds that inhabit the rich biodiversity of Indiana Dunes National Park and Lakeshore, look for the book by Kenneth J. Brock titled Birds of the Indiana Dunes. The former professor of geology wrote this highly-regarded companion for bird watchers who are visiting the region. The data explains which birds are found in the area and when to find them.

28. GIBSON WOODS NATURE PRESERVE

Lake County, Indiana has ten parks and facilities in the Lake County Parks and Rec system. These county parks and nature preserves are home to habitats that attract birds and bird watchers alike. From common waterfowl like the mallard duck to a variety of warblers, there is plenty to see at the parks.

The Gibson Woods Nature Preserve in Hammond, Indiana has an environmental awareness center and private bird room for the education of the species that come to the preserve. Scientists will conduct bird counts at this location during migration season and twice during winter for the backyard bird count.

29. JASPER-PULASKI FISH AND WILDLIFE AREA

Medaryville, Indiana is the location for Jasper-Pulaski Fish and Wildlife Area. The marshlands, prairie, and open fields attract the largest annual migration of the sandhill cranes. It is not unusual to find between 10,000 and 15,000 of the cranes stopping for a rest along with the Northern Harrier and the Rough-Legged Hawk. Sunrise and sunset from the observation tower are the best times to view the cranes during late fall and early spring.

30. KANKAKEE STATE FISH AND WILDLIFE AREA

Kankakee State FWA was once the Kankakee Grand Marsh before most of it was drained for agriculture. Today what is left of the open water, riparian woodlands, and marshes along with the junction of the Yellow River with the Kankakee River. These habitats attract birds such as wild turkey as well as birds of prey like hawks, owls, osprey, and eagles. Other species are attracted to the abundance of cover and food supply of the FWA site, but this location is best known for the waterfowl that spend time here.

31. YELLOWSTONE STATE FOREST

Warbler enthusiasts have an excellent chance to find 18 species of warblers found in Indiana at the Yellowstone State Forest in Brown County, Indiana. This includes the more elusive Cerulean warbler. Since warblers are insect feeders, they are not typically found in more common backyards.

Yellowstone State Forest is located near Brown County State Park. Warblers as well as other migrating birds stop in this south-central part of the state for rest or winter nesting. About 180 species have been spotted amid the ravines and ridgetops.

32. BIG OAK NATIONAL WILDLIFE REFUGE

If sparrows are your interest, Big Oak National Wildlife Refuge will not disappoint. This location near Madison, Indiana is a former Army munitions testing facility. Today it has one of the largest populations of Henslow's Sparrow in their grasslands area during the spring migration. The Henslow's Sparrow is near threatened due to habitat loss on the breeding grounds, conservation efforts from wildlife reserves such as Big Oak are important to restore their population.

The Henslow's sparrow is not the only resident or visitor to the wildlife refuge. More than 120 birds nest at this location while more than 200 pass through during their migration. The Cerulean warbler is one of those birds who find their way to these grounds.

33. MUSCATATUCK

Near Big Oak is Muscatatuck National Wildlife Refuge. At this location near Seymour, Indiana, more than 280 bird species have been counted. As a refuge in south-central Indiana, they are in the middle of the migration path as well as home to numerous birds that will spend the winter on their site.

Environmental education is one of the services that Muscatatuck offers. There are workshops for young and old as well as guided bird walks. Students in the area are familiar with these programs and field trips.

34. GOOSE POND FISH AND WILDLIFE AREA

Indiana's rarest bird, the black-necked stilt can be found in the marsh and prairie habitats found at Goose Pond FWA near Linton,

Indiana in the southwestern portion of the state. Though this bird is typically found near the Pacific coastlines, they can be spotted along with more than 260 bird species. Turkey, dove, and other migratory waterfowl are easy to see as well.

Goose Pond is considered an important breeding and migratory stopover location. Even large birds such as the Sandhill cranes, whooping cranes, and American pelicans will make a stop for rest either to or from their northern breeding grounds. Whooping cranes are endangered with about 800 cranes worldwide but showing signs of a comeback.

Winter is ideal for raptor sightings like the golden eagle, rough-legged hawk, or short-eared owl. There are bird watching hotspots, particularly the visitors center.

35. HOOSIER NATIONAL FOREST

Another south-central area of Indiana is the Hoosier National Forest. As the landscape changes the further south travelers go, the land gives shelter for songbirds that depend on the forest. According to the Audubon Society, this national forest supports the largest population of breeding neotropical migratory birds in Indiana. These birds are the species that breed as far north as Canada in the summer and migrate as far south as South America in the winter. The "neotropic" reference means that they breed north of the Tropic of Cancer (23 degrees north of the equator) and winter south of the Tropic of Cancer. Some of these birds are traveling great distances up to 10,000 miles one way.

Over 140 species of birds have been spotted at Hoosier National Forest. At the Paw Paw Marsh Watchable Wildlife Site, heron and egrets are often visible while winter songbirds are close by. Buzzard Roost looks over the Ohio River with hawks and vultures soaring on air currents. Maines Pond is an ecosystem of open grasslands and small woodlots. This area is desirable for meadowlarks and bluebirds as well as ground-foraging birds like wild turkey and quail.

36. PIGEON RIVER FISH AND WILDLIFE AREA

Not far from Fort Wayne is Pigeon River FWA in Mongo, Indiana. The Pigeon River is just a part of the lake and open-water wetland environment that is open for outdoor opportunities. Waterfowl along with quail, dove, pheasant and wild turkey are often found in this area. Owls such as the Great Horned Owl and Eastern Screech Owl can be heard but not as easy to spot. Migratory birds including warblers are common as are cold-weather residents like winter finches and sparrows. Spring and fall are the best times to see the wild variety of birds in this area.

37. TURKEY RUN STATE PARK

Turkey Run State Park is a popular vacation spot for camping or outdoor getaway, but it is also a great place for bird watching. The interpretive nature center hosts programs all year long. The wildlife watching room gives visitors the opportunity to view the park's inhabitants behind one-way glass windows. Check with the park for the Nature Center's hours of operation.

A unique feature about Turkey Run is its geology. Hiking trails go through canyons within sandstone cliffs along creeks. The different ecosystems of woodlands, streams, and cliffs offer food and shelter possibilities for many species. Morning is a good time to watch turkey vultures, herons, and kingfishers. Walk carefully along the rugged trails when trying to find kinglets, tanagers, and thrushes. During the winter, there are fewer campers and visitors that can distract the birds. Bald eagles are known to roost in this area or just pass by.

38. SUMMIT LAKE STATE PARK

Summit Lake in New Castle, Indiana has recreation for humans and wildlife alike. Waterfowl is abundant here due to the wet meadows and prairies that attract them. Migrating birds also enjoy a break in these parts. Some of the more rare migratory birds have been seen in the park. Sandhill crane, American bittern, least bittern, osprey and bald eagle are just a few of the birds sighted. Bird watching is ideal along the self-guided nature trail through the prairie grass and along the boardwalk in the wetlands before finishing with a view of Summit Lake.

39. CANE RIDGE / GIBSON LAKE

Cane Ridge Station at Gibson Lake is a remote state park near Owensville, Indiana near the Illinois border. Gibson Lake is actually a cooling reservoir for a power generation station nearby. The warm water discharge attracts birds in the winter because other locations are frozen over. This location is maintained by the Cane Ridge Wildlife Management Area as an Important Bird Area because it is the only place where interior Least Tern nest in the Midwest. As a result of their actions, the least tern is no longer on the endangered species list.

Other birds nest at Cane Ridge/Gibson Lake. The Wilson's Phalaropes, black-necked stilts, and bald eagles have been recorded here as well as different egrets and herons. In some places where nesting grounds are becoming developed or taken for agriculture, these nature preserves and wildlife management areas ensure that these birds have a chance to grow and survive.

40. EAGLE CREEK PARK

If you had to narrow down your bird watching experience to one location in Indiana, the birding hotspot would be Eagle Creek Park. The park itself in the capital of Indianapolis has all of the ideal habitats that attract migratory and year-round birds like loons, herons and eagles. However, it is the Ornithology Center at Eagle Creek Park that attracts over 70,000 visitors a year.

The observation deck has great viewing around the park and an outdoor bird checklist to learn more about the birds they have spotted. The Outdoor Migration Game is an interactive educational area outside of the Center to help understand the obstacles birds face. While they are popular during long migration seasons (August to November in the fall, February to April in the spring), Eagle Creek has year-round bird watching experience and bird conservation

awareness programs.

HOW TO SEE BIRDS IN INDIANA

*Everyone likes birds. What wild creature is
more accessible to our eyes and ears, as close to
us and everyone in the world, as universal as a
bird?*

- David Attenborough

41. BACKYARDS

Your Indiana yard can be a sanctuary for you and backyard birds.
How you landscape it can attract or discourage aviary visitors.

Native plants are a great start to attract birds. They are also
adapted to the soil and weather conditions. Insect-loving birds like
sparrows, warblers, and chickadees will enjoy blackberry or
raspberry thickets. Seed-loving birds such as the cardinal, tanager,
and grosbeak are attracted to sunflowers. Elderberry flowers attract
insects as well as birds in the spring and the berries are ready to
harvest between August and September for the fall migration

Trees offer protective cover from larger predators and ideal
nesting areas for some birds. The type of tree will attract different
birds.

- Fruit trees. Small trees that blossom in the spring and bear fruit in the fall attract common backyard birds such as American robin, Northern cardinal, and waxwings to start. Songbirds will sing their praises when fruits and berries start to ripen. Your yard will be fragrant as well as beautiful. Avoid planting these trees close to sidewalks or over patios as rotten fruit and bird droppings will require more labor before you can enjoy the same space.

- Coniferous trees. Evergreen trees like spruce and red cedar provide excellent cover and year-round color. Seed-bearing cones are food when the fall and winter berries die off. If you are looking for the variety with berries, let your nursery expert help you find a female tree.

- Vines. The draping effect of vines can bring a different effect to your backyard. Wild grapes climbing a trellis or a Virginia creeper around a tree will bear fruits in the fall. At the same time, the shredding bark on a grape vine makes excellent nesting material.

- Shrubs. Shrubs such as winterberry or red-osier dogwood are hardy plants that require less maintenance than many plants in a backyard garden. They may need trimming or pruning from time to time. Thrushes, catbirds, and even some migrating warblers may stop for a while and visit.

42. RETENTION PONDS

New housing neighborhoods and commercial areas include a retention pond to collect rain runoff to reduce flooding in the areas. These water features also attract birds, especially waterfowl. Canadian geese and mallard ducks are just a few of the birds that take up residence by the water. Some will rest for a period, but others will feel welcomed and build nests.

If you want to encourage wildlife neighbors to your pond (and it is ok with any HOA or human neighbors), the Cornell Cooperative Extension has some tips to see birds and share your outdoor living space.

- Cut your grass but don't edge mow by the water's edge.
- Add nesting structures such as bird houses on a post or nesting boxes
- If possible, add features such as sunning rocks or fallen logs

Backyard birds and even water birds such as herons, cranes and egrets will start congregating in your neighborhood or at urban ponds near shopping centers and stores. The quieter the setting, the more likely they will come and stay a while. They may also return each season knowing they have a resting place during migration.

43. MISSISSIPPI FLYWAYS

Flyways are the path of migration for birds moving from one location to another based on food and habitat conditions. What amazes scientists is how birds intuitively know where to go year after year without a map or a previous experience of going to this place. Their bodies know that they need to find warmer weather, more abundant food sources, or simply put, a place where they have a better chance to survive.

So how do they find their winter homes? Birds will take flyways, or air paths where other birds are traveling. They don't use a compass, but they do navigate using landmarks. One huge landmark that birds cannot miss is Lake Michigan. Once they find the lake, it doesn't matter if they fly south, southeast, or southwest. Like a funnel, they are flying into Indiana and finding habitats that meet their resting needs and food sources that give them energy to continue their journey.

There are names for the different flyways from Canada to Mexico. Indiana is part of the Mississippi Flyway. Other geological landmarks like the Missouri, Ohio, and Mississippi Rivers guide birds on their migratory path. Millions of ducks, geese, swans, and other birds of all shapes and sizes will travel via the Mississippi Flyway in one season.

44. CITIZEN SCIENTIST EVENTS

Data is an important component in bird studies, yet bird experts and professionals cannot be everywhere at once. You don't have to be an ornithologist to assist in bird data collection. Organizations reach out to citizen scientists. A citizen scientist is an individual who volunteers their time in one way or another. It can be bird species counting or reporting a sick or dead bird in an area. There may be a little bit of training required, but for the most part it is about following directions.

There are often events in which citizen scientists can help gather and analyze data. Bird watching non-profit organizations such as the National Audubon Society or Cornell Lab of Ornithology coordinate events where the number of volunteers contribute to their studies regarding changes in bird populations and behaviors.

The National Audubon Society has conducted the Christmas Bird Count event for more than 100 years. Between December 15 and January 5, beginners and seasoned watchers alike can meet to count the birds they see and hear in a designated area. The Indiana

Audubon Society has over 50 locations for the annual Christmas Bird Count. Indiana Dunes has two different events. State and county parks may post events and may include lunch for the participants.

45. GLOBALLY IMPORTANT BIRD AREAS

An Important Bird Area, or IBA is a designation made by BirdLife International that is significant to the conservation of birds and their habitats. These locations, about 13,000 worldwide, focus on conservation action, planning, and advocacy. IBAs are owned and maintained by the U.S. Forest Service. Visitors are allowed and events may be organized as part of their educational outreach and advocacy efforts, while some areas are prohibited to ensure the health and safety of certain ecosystems.

In Indiana there are 41 IBAs, some of them area Globally Important Bird Areas, or GIBAs which have a higher priority:

• Big Oaks National Wildlife Refuge is designated a GIBA for the Henslow's sparrow. These birds are endangered in the state and Big Oaks is a major breeding ground for them and other birds that migrate through this area. Refuge lands like Big Oaks are carefully maintained for biological integrity, biodiversity, and environmental health.

- Hoosier National Forest is designated an IBA with 8 birds on the Watch list such as red-headed woodpecker, wood thrush, blue-winged warbler, prairie warbler, cerulean warbler, worm-eating warbler, Louisiana waterthrush, and Kentucky warbler. This area is important to migrating neo-tropical birds as breeding grounds.

- Cane Ridge/Gibson Lake is designated an IBA because it is one of two breeding grounds for interior Least Tern birds. It is a habitat for many wintering birds breeding areas due to the warm water discharge from Cinergy's Gibson Generating Station. Other nests for uncommon birds are also built here including the Wilson's Phalaropes and black-necked stilts. Bald eagles, which are protected by the Bald and Golden Eagle Protection Act.

46. WINTER NESTING

Common backyard birds are the ones that are year-round residents of the state. That is why they are visible at bird feeders when there is snow on the ground. They preen their feathers to keep them dry. Geese, ducks, and other waterfowl may stay as long as possible until the ponds and lakes freeze over. Owls like the snowy owl, the largest owl in Indiana, as well as hawks can be heard earlier in the day when the sun sets. They find their prey where possible, including some of the songbirds that are still around.

Birds can prepare for winter by storing food in their tree cavities. Chickadees and blue jays will cache food like acorns and still be able to find them when they are hungry. Backyard feeders with suet or black oil sunflower seeds give birds more energy to generate body heat. Birdhouses and fresh water will keep these backyard birds close by.

Northern Indiana is known for migratory birds coming through the Mississippi Flyway over Lake Michigan, but some may prolong their stay as long as the weather holds. Lake effect snow is likely along Lake Michigan, so more vulnerable birds leave the "snow belt" zone. If a bird is around for the first snow, they may head south so that they don't have to experience a second round of snow, especially if unprepared.

The southern part of the state has more of the breeding grounds during winter and warmer resources for nesting. This is when bald eagles are more likely to be present. Birds from the north like the bobolink will spend their winters in the southern habitats of Indiana such as Hoosier National Forest.

Statewide, the Christmas Bird Count provides researchers with the data. They can see how the population numbers are doing and if there are new birds staying behind to brave the weather or leaving for warmer nesting grounds. The count gives information about migration patterns and climate changes.

47. BIRD WATCHING FESTIVALS AND WALKS

Indiana is a bird watching hotspot, and there are events year round to prove it. Most of the bird watching events and festivals occur during spring and fall migrations.

Muscatatack has the Wings of Muscatatuck Festival during the second weekend in May which coincides with the International Migratory Bird Day weekend. Bird walks, tours, and live sessions are some of the activities for visitors. Indiana Dunes also holds a bird festival around the same time.

Eagle Creek Park has events all year long. The Owl Fest fundraiser comes at an appropriate time in October. Every Sunday morning for two hours they offer a free bird walk led by the Amos Butler Audubon Society. Rain or shine, walkers can observe different species in this city park with expert guidance. This walk is one of the longest-running guided bird walks in the country.

Sunday morning is a popular walking time at Pokagon State Park in Angola, Indiana. Sightings include the red-headed woodpecker or migratory birds depending on the time of year you visit.

The best way to find events is to visit the website of the parks and preserves near where you will be. They will have a list of ongoing activities, annual events, or other pertinent information such as closures or times.

48. INDIANA BIRDING TRAIL

Visitors to Indiana who want to be a part of the bird watching experience, especially during the migration seasons, can find a list of birding trails and resources for the state. The Indiana Birding Trail website has search options for trails including an interactive map that breaks it down by habitat (wetlands, forest, grasslands or open water).

Birding trails are also categorized by regions. That means if you are heading toward Lake Michigan, you can find the different parks, big or small, along with bird watching tips and directions. Total birding time and recommendations make it easy to plan an excursion. Birding guides are also available for hire whether it is for individuals or groups. These regional experts can make the experience even more rewarding.

To find the birding trail information for Indiana, go to Indianabirdingtrail.com to locate the parks, sanctuaries, and other key locations for your best bird watching experience. The Indiana Birding Trail's website is updated and maintained by the Indiana Audubon Society.

49. BIRD ASSOCIATIONS AND EXPERTS

Bird watching can be an individual hobby, but there are benefits when sharing a similar interest with others. Bird associations bring bird enthusiasts of all levels together. They can hold events, raise money to support conservation efforts, and volunteer their time and knowledge to help all birds or particular species. Their resources can also provide assistance to beginners, even junior bird watchers who share the same level of wonder and awe about birds.

- National Audubon Society. The National Audubon Society is a non-profit organization that focuses on protecting the birds and their habitats utilizing science, advocacy, education, and conservation efforts at the source. The organization is named after John James Audubon, the American ornithologist whose illustrated book The Birds of America is acclaimed for its detail of the subject. At a national level, the Audubon Society has 23 state programs, 41 centers, and over 450 chapters. Indiana alone has 11 chapters, and one sanctuary located in Mishawaka. The Indiana Audubon chapters hold events during migration season as well as coordinate many Christmas Bird Counts.

- Cornell Lab of Ornithology. The Cornell Lab of Ornithology is a non-profit organization affiliated with Cornell University's College of Agriculture and Life Sciences. Data from avian population studies is a huge part of their involvement, but also the advancement of technology along with education and on-the-ground conservation. They want to protect nature and preserve the bird population as well as create a more sustainable planet for humans. Though the lab is based in Ithaca, New York, their projects and resources are accessible worldwide.

- American Birding Association. The American Birding Association (ABA) is a non-profit organization for recreational birding in North America. Since 1969, the ABA has followed their mission to inspire all people to enjoy and protect wild birds. They do this by providing resources and hold workshops and camps for the young and old. The group conducts a Big Day Count in order to identify as many bird species during a single calendar day by all team members of the ABA. The organization has their own Code of Birding Ethics and encourages birders not only to enjoy watching birds, but promote conservation for their habitats.

- BirdLife International. BirdLife is a global partnership of independent organizations that work together for nature and people. They focus on local challenges that promote lasting solutions. Their impact on Indiana is the identification, documentation, and protection of the Important Bird and Biodiversity Areas (IBAs). This conservation partnership allows to protect habitats for breeding and nesting birds that are losing habitats due to poor management and development. There are 41 IBAS in Indiana that cover over 731,000 acres of land.

50. BIRD WATCHING APPS

The Audubon Bird Guide app aids bird watchers in identifying more than 800 birds and their songs. It also features a checklist to record sighted birds. The field guide is accessible without wifi in case of no service areas out in the remote habitats. For all of the expertise and resources, this app is free to download on the App Store and Google Play.

Cornell Lab of Ornithology also has their own free bird app called Merlin Bird ID. It helps identify more than 600 birds in the U.S. and Canada as well as plays sounds and videos. There is life history of birds along with interesting facts and maps on where to find them. Possible matches are made with three simple questions. All bird finds can be saved on a life list called Save My Bird. This app is available for download on the App Store and Google Play.

The IBird Pro Guide is an interactive pocket guide for birders. It was the first app for bird watchers when the App store opened in 2008. It has multiple illustrations and maps to help identify birds by sight. The large sound library assists with bird calls. The iBird Lite app is free, but the full app is not. There are in-app purchase features including Photo Sleuth for tough photo identifications and Birds Around Me for GPS matches in a narrow radius. This app is available for download on the App Store and Google Play.

eBird is a free, easy-to-use app for bird tracking. You record your observations on your checklist with GPS enabled location plotting. If the bird you spied is a rare sighting, you get real-time feedback. Your findings do more than just check boxes on your watch list. It actually adds it to a global online database for other birders and is available for scientific research, education, and conservation. As a tool for citizen scientist goals, this app takes little effort from you. It is available for download on the App Store and Google Play.

If you want to volunteer for bird counts but do not feel confident in your bird song identification, the Larkwire app makes a game out of it. By downloading song packs for different regions (Eastern/ Central North America or Western North America), you can train your ear to identify more than 200 species per region. This app is available on the App Store or online with the web version.

Song Sleuth takes the guesswork out of song identification. This free app identifies, records, and shares recordings while providing additional facts about the birds you hear. Song Sleuth can identify over 200 bird species and let you know how common they are. This app was created in collaboration with ornithologist and bird illustration David Sibley. It is available for download on the App Store and Google Play.

Want something for a specific species? There are apps based on particular finds including The Warbler Guide and Raptor ID.

OTHER HELPFUL RESOURCES

Audubon Society - www.audubon.org

Cornell Lab of Ornithology - www.birds.cornell.edu

Indiana Birding Trail - www.indianabirdingtrail.com

Eagle Creek Park - eaglecreekpark.org/ornithology-center/

World Birds: Joy of Nature - worldbirds.com

BOOKS IN PRINT

For more information about birds in Indiana, there are print books that are great field guides for beginning and expert birders.

Brock, Kenneth J. Birds of the Indiana Dunes: Revised Edition 1997

Peterson, Roger Tory. Peterson Field Guide to Birds of North America 2020

READ OTHER
50 THINGS TO KNOW ABOUT BIRDS IN THE UNITED STATES BOOKS

50 Things to Know About Birds in Illinois

50 Things to Know About Birds in Missouri

50 Things to Know About Birds in New York

50 Things to Know About Birds in Oklahoma

50 Things to Know About Birds in Oregon

50 Things to Know About Birds in Pennsylvania

50 Things to Know

Stay up to date with new releases on Amazon:

https://amzn.to/2VPNGr7

CZYKPublishing.com

50 Things to Know

We'd love to hear what you think about our content! Please leave your honest review of this book on Amazon and Goodreads. We appreciate your positive and constructive feedback. Thank you.